*Nothing can bring you peace
but yourself.*

— *Ralph Waldo Emerson*

Blue Mountain Arts®

New and Best-Selling Titles

By Susan Polis Schutz:
To My Daughter with Love on the Important Things in Life
To My Son with Love

By Douglas Pagels:
For You, My Soul Mate
May You Be Blessed with All These Things
Required Reading for All Teenagers

By Marci:
Friends Are Forever
10 Simple Things to Remember
To My Daughter
You Are My "Once in a Lifetime"

By Wally Amos, with Stu Glauberman:
The Path to Success Is Paved with Positive Thinking

By M. Butler and D. Mastromarino:
Take Time for You

By James Downton, Jr.:
Today, I Will... Words to Inspire Positive Life Changes

By Donna Fargo:
I Thanked God for You Today

By Carol Wiseman:
Emerging from the Heartache of Loss

Anthologies:
A Daughter Is Life's Greatest Gift
A Sister's Love Is Forever
A Son Is Life's Greatest Gift
Dream Big, Stay Positive, and Believe in Yourself
Friends for Life
God Is Always Watching Over You
Hang In There
Keep Believing in Yourself and Your Dreams
The Love Between a Mother and Daughter Is Forever
There Is Nothing Sweeter in Life Than a Granddaughter
The Strength of Women
Think Positive Thoughts Every Day
Words Every Woman Should Remember

The
Peace

Within You

Calming Thoughts to Help You

Slow Down, Let Go,

and Discover Your Inner Joy

Edited by
Patricia Wayant

Blue Mountain Press™

Boulder, Colorado

We wish to thank Susan Polis Schutz for permission to reprint the following poems that appear in this publication: "There Is So Much to Be Thankful For." Copyright © 1990 by Stephen Schutz and Susan Polis Schutz. And for "We need to feel more...." Copyright © 1972 by Continental Publications. Renewed © 2000 by Stephen Schutz and Susan Polis Schutz. All rights reserved.

Library of Congress Control Number: 2012955492
ISBN: 978-1-59842-708-0

⚔ and Blue Mountain Press are registered in U.S. Patent and Trademark Office.
Certain trademarks are used under license.

Acknowledgments appear on page 92.

Printed in China.
Second Printing: 2014

♲ This book is printed on recycled paper.

This book is printed on paper that has been specially produced to be acid free (neutral pH) and contains no groundwood or unbleached pulp. It conforms with the requirements of the American National Standards Institute, Inc., so as to ensure that this book will last and be enjoyed by future generations.

Blue Mountain Arts, Inc.
P.O. Box 4549, Boulder, Colorado 80306

Contents
(Authors listed in order of first appearance)

Within you there is a stillness, a haven to which you can withdraw at any time and be at home there.

— Hermann Hesse

Slow Down, Let Go, and Discover Your Inner Joy

The world will not fall apart
or leave you behind
if you allow yourself
a few moments of quiet.

There is no need for stress
and struggle.
Everything that is meant to be
will be —
with or without your help.

So relax,
find your balance,
and remember…
breathe.

— Lisa Butler

Live in the Moment

To be in the moment means
to sit in reflection, in silence,
allowing for thoughts and emotions
to flow freely.
It means to take a breather
from your everyday schedule
to enjoy the simple things in life.

To be in the moment means
not letting life pass you by.
It allows you to experience
each moment for what it is
and then let it go
like a feather floating in the wind.

To be in the moment allows us
to see the many blessings we have —
the wonderful gifts
that we so quickly look past
in our day-to-day lives.
It means truly and entirely living.

— Lamisha Serf

The Six Most Important Things You Can Do

🍃 Look in the mirror and smile... and see an amazing person looking back at you. You really are someone special, and your presence is a present to the world around you.

🍃 When you're counting your blessings, be sure to include the privilege of having a new sunrise every morning and a brand-new beginning every day.

🍃 Don't ever give up on your hopes and dreams. Your happiness is depending on you to stay strong.

🍃 Know that you can reach deep inside
and find everything you need to get
through each moment that lies ahead.

🍃 When you talk to those who matter
most, open the door to your heart. The
wider it is, the easier it will be for things
like compassion and understanding
to come inside. And it just naturally
follows… the more wonderful visitors
you have, the more your life will shine.

🍃 Have simple pleasures in this complex
world. Be a joyous spirit and a sensitive
soul. Take those long walks that would
love to be taken. Explore those sunlit
paths that would love to oblige. Don't
just have minutes in the day; have
moments in time.

— Douglas Pagels

Life Is Simply
a Journey

As you traverse life's diverse pathways,
you will encounter many obstacles,
some good and some bad.
All are learning experiences.

Life is simply a journey,
and we all start at the beginning.
Embrace everything life has to offer;
you never know when
the journey will end.

For some their time
spent on enlightenment is short,
for others it's long,
but it is up to each of us
to work out our own direction.

No one knows what is right for another —
it is hard enough to know
what is right for ourselves.
Try to understand others,
or at least make allowances for them.
Their journeys may be
more arduous than yours.

There are no failures and no successes,
only lessons learned.

— Gary Seymour

Take It Slow and Easy

Never be in a hurry; do everything quietly and in a calm spirit. Do not lose your inward peace for anything whatsoever, even if your whole world seems upset.

— Francis de Sales

There is no joy but calm.

— Alfred Lord Tennyson

Being calm is easy:
calm cannot be seen,
calm cannot be heard,
calm cannot be held.

Calm can be felt
both inside and out.
It rests in the moments
before dawn
and just after sleep.
A sunset holds us
in its calm as the sun slips
below our horizon.

You can be calm
in your own rising
and setting.
You can be calm
in your everyday life.

— Pamela Metz

One Day at a Time

Our lives are made up of a million moments, spent in a million different ways. Some are spent searching for love, peace, and harmony. Others are spent surviving day to day. But there is no greater moment than when we find that life — with all its joys and sorrows — is meant to be lived one day at a time.

It's in this knowledge that we discover the most wonderful truth of all. Whether we live in a forty-room mansion, surrounded by servants and wealth, or find it a struggle to manage the rent month to month, we have it within our power to be fully satisfied and live a life with true meaning.

— Regina Hill

One day at a time —
this is enough.
Do not look back
and grieve over the past,
for it is gone;
and do not be troubled
about the future,
for it has not yet come.
Live in the present,
and make it so beautiful
that it will be worth
remembering.

— Ida Scott Taylor

The Serenity Prayer

God grant me the serenity
to accept the things
I cannot change;
the courage to change
the things I can;
and the wisdom
to know the difference.

— Reinhold Niebuhr

We cannot change the past;
we just need to keep
the good memories
and acquire wisdom
from the mistakes we've made.
We cannot predict the future;
we just need to hope and pray
for the best and what is right,
and believe that's how it will be.
We can live a day at a time,
enjoying the present
and always seeking to become
a more loving and better person.

— Karen Berry

Acceptance

Acceptance means that you
      can find the serenity within
to let go of the past
      with its mistakes and regrets,
move into the future
      with a new perspective,
and appreciate the opportunity
      to take a second chance.

Acceptance means that when
      difficult times come into your life,
you'll find security again and comfort
      to relieve any pain.
You'll find new dreams, fresh hopes,
      and forgiveness of the heart.

Acceptance does not mean
    that you will always be perfect.
It simply means that
    you'll always overcome imperfection.

Acceptance is the road to peace —
    letting go of the worst,
holding on to the best,
    and finding the hope inside
that continues throughout life.

Acceptance is the heart's best defense,
    love's greatest asset,
and the easiest way to keep believing
    in yourself and others.

— Regina Hill

Look Within

Within yourself lies the cause of whatever enters into your life. To come into the full realization of your own awakened interior powers is to be able to condition your life in exact accord with what you would have it.

— Ralph Waldo Trine

What lies behind us and what lies before us are tiny matters compared to what lies within us.

— Ralph Waldo Emerson

Listen to your inner voice;
it is the most important connection
    between your head and heart.
Leave self-doubt behind;
it serves only to make you hesitate.
Never stop questioning, searching,
    and reaching;
they are the only ways to stretch
your mind and soul.
No matter what you do in this life,
remember it is never about
    the treasures you acquire;
it's about making certain
it is <u>life</u> you treasure.

— Lisa Crofton

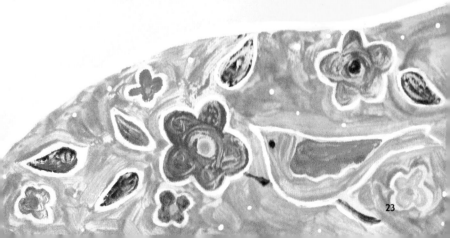

Oh, the thousands of men and women all about us weary with care, troubled and ill at ease, running hither and thither to find peace, weary in body, soul, and mind; going to other countries, traveling the world over, coming back, and still not finding it. Of course they have not found it and they never will find it in this way, because they are looking for it where it is not. They are looking for it without when they should look within. Peace is to be found only within, and unless one finds it there, he will never find it at all.

— Ralph Waldo Trine

Beyond your challenges, beyond your successes, beyond the events with which life has molded your spirit, there is a placeless place within you. It is a place of peace. It is a place of freedom. It is the place where the Self you have been seeking resides.

— Barbara De Angelis, PhD

Discover the Calm of Quietness

There is something greater and purer than what the mouth utters. Silence illuminates our souls, whispers to our hearts, and brings them together. Silence separates us from ourselves, makes us sail the firmament of spirit, and brings us closer to Heaven; it makes us feel that bodies are no more than prisons and that this world is only a place of exile.

— Kahlil Gibran

One should clean out a room in one's home and place only a tea table and a chair in the room with some boiled water and fragrant tea. Afterward, sit salutarily and allow one's spirit to become tranquil, light, and natural.

— Li Ri Hua

Learn to get in touch with the silence within yourself and know that everything in this life has a purpose. There are no mistakes, no coincidences, all events are blessings given to us to learn from.

— Elisabeth Kübler-Ross

Mowing

There was never a sound beside the wood but one,
And that was my long scythe whispering to the ground.
What was it it whispered? I knew not well myself;
Perhaps it was something about the heat of the sun,
Something, perhaps, about the lack of sound —
And that was why it whispered and did not speak.
It was no dream of the gift of idle hours,
Or easy gold at the hand of fay or elf:
Anything more than the truth would have
     seemed too weak
To the earnest love that laid the swale in rows,
Not without feeble-pointed spikes of flowers
(Pale orchises), and scared a bright green snake.
The fact is the sweetest dream that labor knows.
My long scythe whispered and left the hay to make.

— Robert Frost

The Peace of Wild Things

When despair for the world grows in me
and I wake in the night at the least sound
in fear of what my life and my children's lives may be,
I go and lie down where the wood drake
rests in his beauty on the water,
    and the great heron feeds.
I come into the peace of wild things
who do not tax their lives with forethought
of grief. I come into the presence of still water.
And I feel above me the day-blind stars
waiting with their light. For a time
I rest in the grace of the world, and am free.

— Wendell Berry

Solitude

I would have all busy people make times in their lives... when they should try to be alone with nature and their own hearts. They should try to realize the quiet, unwearying life that manifests itself in field and wood. They should wander alone in solitary places where the hazel-hidden stream makes music and the bird sings out of the heart of the forest; in meadows where the flowers grow brightly... I will go further and say that a man who does not wish to do these things is shutting one of the doors of his spirit, a door through which many sweet and true things come in.

— Arthur C. Benson

Settle into yourself
Be truly alone

And not the kind of alone
that makes your heart sore
but the kind that causes
your breath to slow
your limbs to go weightless
your thoughts to fall from you
one by one

Embrace the moment
that leaves you in
complete solitude
Welcome these times
as a gift of peace
for your spirit and soul

Your sustenance

— Elle Mastro

A Simple Lesson in Mindfulness

This is a very short and simple lesson in mindfulness, a way in which we can bring peace to ourselves in any moment. Practicing this twenty minutes each day, preferably in the morning, will change your life.

Sit comfortably, with your back as straight as possible. Let your entire body relax. Close your eyes very gently. Bring your full awareness to your breath as you breathe in and out through your nose. You can say to yourself: "I am breathing in. I am breathing out. In. Out." Or: "I am breathing in peace. I am breathing out tension. Peace. Tension."

Simply notice whatever takes you from your breathing — a thought, sound, itch, daydream — and acknowledge it by naming it. Then, very gently, without judgment, go back to your breathing.

By practicing this twenty minutes in the morning, every day, you will learn how powerful your breath is, and you will become more and more aware that you can turn to your breath at any time during the day to bring peace to your heart.

— Ruth Fishel

When I dance I dance; when I sleep I sleep; yes, when I walk alone in a beautiful orchard, if my thoughts have been concerned with extraneous incidents for some part of the time, for some other part I lead them back again to the walk, to the orchard, to the sweetness of solitude, and to myself.

— Michel de Montaigne

Find Your Center

Whenever you sense a feeling that is not harmonious, peaceful, and loving — all of which are your nature — you know you are out of alignment. So pause for a moment. Recognize this is not who you are or who you want to be. Take a deep breath and stop. You always have the power to pause at any moment.

— Mary Manin Morrissey

Flow with whatever is happening and let your mind be free. Stay centered by accepting whatever you are doing. This is the ultimate.

— Zhuangzi

Mind and body
Together,
Thoughts and emotions
Revolving around
A single center point.
Varied movements
Actively churning
From a quiet center.
A quiet center forms
In their midst.

We feel the center of our Self,
The inner center of our Self,
It is neither body
Nor mind
But a center point
Not this, not that,
A single center point,
The inner center of the Self.

— Ira Progoff

Let Go...

Let go...
  of guilt; it's okay to make
  the same mistakes again.
Let go...
  of obsessions; they seldom
  turn out the way you planned.
Let go...
  of hate; it's a waste of love.
Let go...
  of blaming others; you are
  responsible for your own destiny.
Let go...
  of fantasies; so reality can
  come true.

Let go…
   of self-pity; someone else may
   need you.
Let go…
   of wanting; cherish what you have.
Let go…
   of fear; it's a waste of faith.
Let go…
   of despair; change comes from
   acceptance and forgiveness.
Let go…
   of the past; the future is
   here — right now.

— Kathleen O'Brien

Look for Joy in Small Things

Life can be so busy, and we sometimes take for granted the important little things that make us smile. Look at the sunset, share a cup of coffee with your best friend, or hear the wind rustle through the trees. Take some time to listen to life and feel the sun on your face. Stop to watch butterflies in your garden.

— Carol Schelling

Sometimes it's the little things that mean the most: the song of a bird, a warm breeze blowing through the trees, a friendly voice on the other end of a telephone, a note written by a friend to us when we need encouragement, the wag of a dog's tail as we come home from a hard day at work. These things are intangible — we cannot put a price tag on what they mean to us or how they help us to feel abiding peace even in the midst of turmoil.

— Heather Parkins

Take nothing for granted: the sheer act
of waking each day; fresh air upon your cheek;
each effort expended on self or another —
walking the dog, shopping for food,
toiling at home, in an office, or on the road.
Every moment is rare, short, and full of glory.
Every word is magic;
a story achieved through will.
Marvel at nature's moods as mirror of your own.
Recall a sunrise or sunset,
a flock of geese in the sky.

Care about parents or children as fragile gifts,
like petals on a rose, like songs from one bird.
Praise the simple or complex —
the invention of flight above clouds;
the wheel; the bathtub; a rocking chair.
We rise and fall in the moon or a wave,
in a smile or many tears.
And being brave is to be alive
as we give and share love always,
only and ever to survive.

— Rochelle Lynn Holt

The Power of Simplicity

The trouble with so many of us is that we underestimate the power of simplicity. We have a tendency it seems to overcomplicate our lives and forget what's important and what's not. We tend to mistake movement for achievement. We tend to focus on activities instead of results. And as the pace of life continues to race along in the outside world, we forget that we have the power to control our lives regardless of what's going on outside.

— Robert Stuberg

Simplicity is different from focus, different from balance, different from harmony — although simplifying your days can make the process of focusing and balancing much easier. The process of simplifying your life is primarily the process of making room, clearing out space, and letting some light into the cluttered closets of your days. In a sense, the act of simplifying your life is really the process of giving yourself freedom — freeing mind and schedule from the overload of activities and occupations that inevitably weigh you down.

— Thomas Kinkade

As you begin to live more seriously within, you begin to live more simply without.

— Ralph Waldo Emerson

Things That Matter

Make time in your busy schedule now and then to contemplate and slow way down — to gaze at the landscape, marvel at the beauty and the majesty of the trees, and look up until you can almost touch that big, out-of-reach blue sky. Be thankful you can see.

Be still and hear the sounds around you. Listen to the birds speaking their own language. Hear the universe singing and the world making its music in concert with the rhythms of the traffic. Tune in to those melodies in your heart for inspiration. Be glad you can hear.

Breathe in hope and joy, and feel the life-giving air. Breathe out fear and regret. Don't worry about doing anything this moment except being where you are. Feel the harmony of your relationship with every living thing. Be mindful of the people who are positive influences in your life.

Take the time to fall in love with life with the innocence and wonder of a child.

— Donna Fargo

We Are Each a Part of the Whole

The first peace, which is the most important, is that which comes within the souls of people when they realize their oneness with the universe and all its powers.

— Black Elk

Inner peace comes through working for the good of all. We are all cells in the body of humanity — all of us, all over the world. Each one has a contribution to make, and will know from within what this contribution is, but no one can find inner peace except by working, not in a self-centered way, but for the whole human family.

— Peace Pilgrim

The birds and animals, trees and grasses, rocks, water, and wind are our allies. They waken our senses, rouse our passions, renew our spirits, and fill us with vision, courage, and joy....

As long as the birds return and the flowers bloom, I will dream of a time when we value blue skies more than new automobiles, count our wealth in joy rather than possessions, and dwell in peace and balance with the earth. I am not without hope.

— David Gaines

Grace

To live in a state of grace means to be fully in tune with your spiritual nature and a higher power that sustains you. Grace comes when you are able to move from your lower self, where your ego dictates the path that "should be" rightfully yours, to your higher self, where you are able to transcend your ego and expand into your greater good. It comes when you shift from a "me"-centered reality to an understanding of the bigger picture. Grace comes when you understand and accept that the universe always creates circumstances that lead every person to his or her own true path, and that everything happens for a reason as part of a divine plan....

In the state of grace you trust in yourself
and the universe. You can celebrate other
people's blessings, knowing that their gifts are
right and appropriate for them and that the
universe has your gift right around the corner.

— Chérie Carter-Scott, PhD

Be Gentle with Yourself and Others

We can't always be peaceful and loving, even when we have the best intentions. Unexpected events can stimulate fear. Buttons can be pushed. A burst of anger can lead to words we later regret. No emotion is right or wrong. All emotions are natural.

It is so important that we be gentle with ourselves and accept our emotions without judgment, no matter what is going on. Acceptance releases negative energy.

Just knowing that there are times when we are powerless over our feelings can be the beginning of peace. Turning our emotions over to a power greater than ourselves, and trusting that God can and will do for us what we cannot do for ourselves, can bring us peace.

— Ruth Fishel

Remember to be gentle with yourself and others. We all are children of chance, and none can say why some fields will blossom while others lay brown beneath the August sun.

Care for those around you. Look past your differences. Their dreams are no less than yours, their choices in life no more easily made.

And give. Give in any way you can, of whatever you possess. To give is to love. To withhold is to wither. Care less for your harvest than for how it is shared, and your life will have meaning and your heart will have peace.

— Kent Nerburn

Relax

The gently tapered wings of swift lake swallows cut through the air like soft whispering sighs, while they dart in and out of a clustered hovering mass of mayflies that drift just inches above the shimmering lake that reflects the orange hued light of the setting sun.

On a floating dock, worn in spots by the rubbing of moored boats, I sit in a weathered Adirondack chair with the purpose of only to relax to the rhythmic rocking caused by small rolling waves from cruising pleasure boats, with people waving as they pass by.

Looking down through the clear jade tinted waters
I notice the octagonal amber markings on a small box turtle
that seems to be ambling, rather than swimming, through
the still water as it passes by, seemingly without a care
for anything but its mysterious unknown destination.

These moments pass fleetingly, but remain ingrained in
my mind for those times where I feel the sides pressing
in, my escape is into these simple moments, where all that
the world requires of you is to sit back and take in what
is offered, without asking for anything in return.

— James Bowie

Find Calm in Loving Thoughts

All of us long for peace. We search for it in every way and in every place but in the one way and one place where it must eventually be found. And where is it to be found? In thought that is loving…

Peace isn't separate from you. You are peace. When you think loving thoughts toward others you are peaceful.

— W. Norman Cooper

The Peace Prayer
of St. Francis

Lord make me an instrument of your peace.
Where there is hatred,
Let me sow love;
Where there is injury, pardon;
Where there is error, truth;
Where there is doubt, faith;
Where there is despair, hope;
Where there is darkness, light;
And where there is sadness, joy.

— Author Unknown

I Remember...

I remember when I was young
and driving thirty miles in sixty minutes
of rush hour traffic twice a day so
I could work for eight hours two cities
away from my children in an office
that afforded a view of concrete ribbons
screaming in every direction with
people who knew my name but that's all
and climate control that kept everything
uniform in every season.

I used to think about my grandparents
tucked away in the piney woods in
their small, wooden house with a
screened-in porch for summer sleeping
and their tiny kitchen with a green Formica
table top and a clear plastic cover over
the floral sofa so you could see
the bouquets underneath;

with a vegetable garden and a chicken coop
and a trout pond and an old pickup truck
the oil company gave my grandfather
to drive to check their wells, twice a day,
his job.

I remember them waking up together
and working alongside,
him hoeing the garden while
she did the laundry and sitting down for lunch
together, every day, bowing their heads to
say thanks for the sweet corn and the leftover
fried chicken and the coupons for paper towels
in the newspaper that day and how those
vinyl chairs clung to your flesh
and never wanted to let your legs
go anywhere else.

— Sally Clark

Let Nothing Disturb Your Peace of Mind

We cannot choose how many years we will live, but we can choose how much life those years will have. We cannot control the beauty of our face, but we can control the expression on it. We cannot control life's difficult moments, but we can choose to make life less difficult. We cannot control the negative atmosphere of the world, but we can control the atmosphere of our minds. Too often we try to choose and control things we cannot. Too seldom we choose to control what we can... our attitude.

— Author Unknown

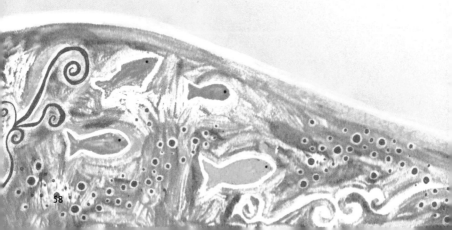

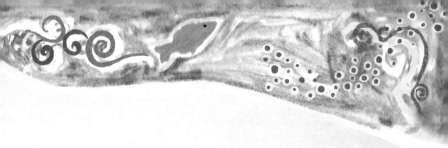

When you are disturbed by events and lose your serenity, quickly return to yourself and don't stay upset longer than the experience lasts; for you'll have more mastery over your inner harmony by continually returning to it.

— Marcus Aurelius

Each one has to find his peace from within. And peace to be real must be unaffected by outside circumstances.

— Mahatma Gandhi

Respond with Serenity

There is no need to give up your serenity for the sake of getting something accomplished. In fact, accomplishment comes more surely when your efforts are calm and your spirit is peaceful.

Consider how very much more you can get done when your energy is not being sapped away by a frenzied mind. True serenity is not the absence of action, but rather action with integrity, confidence, and a steadfastness of purpose.

The world may very well be swirling around you in a constant turmoil. But you don't have to adopt that turmoil as your own.

The more frenzied and hurried life becomes, the more serene and unperturbed you have the opportunity to be. Whatever you can accomplish in a hectic and chaotic state, you can accomplish much more powerfully with peaceful, calm determination.

When you're confronted with turmoil, respond with serenity. It will lift you to a higher level of experience and accomplishment.

— Ralph S. Marston, Jr.

Open Your Heart
to All That Is Beautiful

Never lose an opportunity of seeing
anything that is beautiful; for beauty
is God's handwriting — a wayside
sacrament. Welcome it in every fair face,
in every fair sky, in every fair flower, and
thank God for it as a cup of blessing.

— Ralph Waldo Emerson

The longer I live the more my mind dwells upon the beauty and wonder of the world.... I have loved the feel of the grass under my feet, and the sound of the running streams by my side. The hum of the wind in the treetops has always been good music to me, and the face of the fields has often comforted me more than the faces of men.

I am in love with this world.... I have tilled its soil, I have gathered its harvest, I have waited upon its seasons, and always have I reaped what I have sown.... I have climbed its mountains, roamed its forests, sailed its waters, crossed its deserts, felt the sting of its frosts, the oppression of its heats, the drench of its rains, the fury of its winds, and always have beauty and joy waited upon my goings and comings.

— John Burroughs

In Beauty May I Walk

In beauty may I walk.
All day long may I walk.
Through the returning seasons may I walk.
On the trail marked with pollen may I walk.
With grasshoppers about my feet may I walk.
With dew about my feet may I walk.
With beauty may I walk.
With beauty before me, may I walk.
With beauty behind me, may I walk.
With beauty above me, may I walk.
With beauty below me, may I walk.
With beauty all around me, may I walk.
In old age wandering on a trail of beauty,
    lively, may I walk.
In old age wandering on a trail of beauty,
    living again, may I walk.
It is finished in beauty.
It is finished in beauty.

— Mountain Chant of the Navajo

A walk. The atmosphere incredibly pure — a warm, caressing gentleness in the sunshine — joy in one's whole being.... Forgotten impressions of childhood and youth came back to me — all those indescribable effects wrought by color, shadow, sunlight, green hedges, and songs of birds, upon the soul just opening to poetry. I became young again, wondering, and simple, as candor and ignorance are simple. I abandoned myself to life and to nature, and they cradled me with an infinite gentleness.

— Henry Amiel

Where Joy Resides

Joy is being in love and sleeping in the sunshine and running down a mountain path with the swiftness of a deer in the springtime. Joy expands your heart and opens your soul. Joy is snowflakes and slipping on the ice and getting up so you can slip all over again and never even feeling the cold. Living in joy doesn't mean putting on a happy face. It means that joy is at the core of who you are and always have been.

Joy is strong enough to carry you
through the darkness and the pain
into a place where joy still resides in
ultimate measure. Seek to find joy
and let joy fill your life.

— Rachel Snyder

Dream under a night sky; dance to the light of your own music. Do the things that make your heart sing. Be your own biggest fan. Bask in the glow of your potential. Cherish yourself. Today and every day, take some "me time" just for you... because you're more special than you know.

Celebrate the stars shining in you. Every dawn is a new beginning filled with adventure. Chart your own journey. See yourself as a beautiful person — because you are. Keep your hopes shining bright. There are so many things that make you special. With every step you take, love walks along with you. Have faith in your own wonderful self; you really can do anything you set your mind to.

Chase joy. Run after happiness. The journey you take from here will be as beautiful as you make it. Like morning sunshine, let love come softly to you. Linger under some moonlight. Let it warm you from the inside out. See yourself for the wonderful person you are.

Open your own heart, and let these thoughts bless you today and always.

— Linda E. Knight

The Gratitude Habit

If we knew how much the habit of being thankful might do for us, I am sure we would take time out every day to count up a few of our blessings. When the spirit of thankfulness takes its place in our consciousness, we radiate life from the very center of our being to the world about us.

— Author Unknown

Be grateful for the growing trees,
    the roses soon to bloom,
The tenderness of kindly hearts that
    shared your days of gloom;
Be grateful for the morning dew,
    the grass beneath your feet,
The soft caresses of your babes and
    all their laughter sweet.

Acquire the grateful habit, learn to see
    how blest you are,
How much there is to gladden life,
    how little life to mar!
And what if rain shall fall today and
    you with grief are sad;
Be grateful that you can recall
    the joys that you have had.

                — Edgar A. Guest

There Is So Much to Be Thankful For

We don't often
take the time out of our busy lives
to think about all
the beautiful things
and to be thankful for them
If we did reflect on these things
we would realize how very
lucky and fortunate we really are

I am very thankful
for the love of my husband —
which is so complete and fulfilling
and is based on honesty, equality
intellectualism and romance

I am very thankful
for the love of my children —
which is all encompassing
and is based on teaching, tenderness
sensitivity, caring and hugging

I am very thankful
that I am able to love
and that the love is returned to me

I am very thankful
that I am healthy
and that the people I love
are healthy

I am very thankful
that I have dreams to follow
and goals to strive for

I am very thankful
for the beauty of nature —
magnificent mountains
the colorful leaves
the smell of the flowers
the roaring of the waves
the setting sun
the rising moon

Everywhere I look
I see the wonders of nature
and I feel so proud
to be a small part of it

I am very thankful
for all the good people in the world
I am very thankful
that I have good friends

I am very thankful
to be alive
in a time when
we can make the world
a better place
to live in
— Susan Polis Schutz

Let Love Be Your Guide

Love flows from the beauty
   around us
Love smiles through those
   we hold especially dear
Love speaks soft words
   that help guide us

— Joel Winsome Williams

Each day is an opportunity for a new beginning and a chance to grow and share our hearts, our love, and our lives to the fullest. Sometimes that means just making the most out of the smallest things — like listening to each other, holding each other's hand, or just being together.

— Star Nakamoto

Fill your heart with the kindness of friends, the caring of everyone you love, and the richness of memories you wouldn't trade for anything.

— Douglas Pagels

You will find as you look back upon your life that the moments that stand out, the moments when you have really lived, are the moments when you have done things in a spirit of love.

— Henry Drummond

We need to feel more
to understand others
We need to love more
to be loved back
We need to cry more
to cleanse ourselves
We need to laugh more
to enjoy ourselves

We need to be honest and fair
when interacting with people
We need to establish a strong ethical basis
as a way of life
We need to see more
than our own fantasies
We need to hear more
and listen to the needs of others

We need to give more
and take less
We need to share more
and own less
We need to realize the importance
   of the family
as a backbone to stability
We need to look more
and realize that we are not so
   different from one another

We need to create a world where
we can trust one another
We need to create a world where
we can all peacefully live
the life we choose

            — Susan Polis Schutz

Trust in Yourself, Your Path, and the Universe

Rather than wondering about or questioning the direction your life has taken, accept the fact that there is a path before you now. Shake off the "whys" and "what ifs," and rid yourself of confusion. Whatever was — is in the past. Whatever is — is what's important. The past is a brief reflection. The future is yet to be realized. Today is here.

Walk your path one step at a time — with courage, faith, and determination. Keep your head up and cast your dreams to the stars. Soon your steps will become firm and your footing will be solid again. A path that you never imagined will become the most comfortable direction you could have ever hoped to follow.

Keep your belief in yourself and walk into your new journey. You will find it magnificent, spectacular, and beyond your wildest imaginings.

— Vicki Silvers

Don't be afraid; believe.
Trust that the days ahead will be filled
with peace and strength
and the future will be all
it is meant to be.
I am praying...
I am believing...
Believe with me.

— Rick Norman

Desiderata

Go placidly amid the noise and the haste, and remember what peace there may be in silence. ⚘ As far as possible, without surrender, be on good terms with all persons. Speak your truth quietly and clearly; and listen to others, even to the dull and ignorant; they too have their story. ⚘ Avoid loud and aggressive persons; they are vexatious to the spirit. ⚘ If you compare yourself with others, you may become vain or bitter, for always there will be greater and lesser persons than yourself. ⚘ Enjoy your achievements as well as your plans. Keep interested in your own career, however humble; it is a real possession in the changing fortunes of time. ⚘ Exercise caution in your business affairs, for the world is full of trickery. But let this not blind you to what virtue there is; many persons strive for high ideals, and everywhere life is full of heroism. ⚘

Be yourself. Especially do not feign affection. 🍃 Neither be cynical about love; for in the face of all aridity and disenchantment, it is as perennial as the grass. 🍃 Take kindly the counsel of the years, gracefully surrendering the things of youth. Nurture strength of spirit to shield you in sudden misfortune. But do not distress yourself with dark imaginings. Many fears are born of fatigue and loneliness. 🍃 Beyond a wholesome discipline, be gentle with yourself. 🍃 You are a child of the universe no less than the trees and the stars; you have a right to be here. 🍃 And whether or not it is clear to you, no doubt the universe is unfolding as it should. Therefore be at peace with God, whatever you conceive Him to be. 🍃 And whatever your labors and aspirations, in the noisy confusion of life, keep peace in your soul. 🍃 With all its sham, drudgery and broken dreams, it is still a beautiful world. Be cheerful. Strive to be happy. 🍃

— Max Ehrmann

Life's Most Important Treasures

Joy
   in your heart,
   your mind,
   your soul.
Happiness
   with yourself
   and with the world.
Harmony.
Courage
   to feel, to need,
   to reach out.
Freedom
   to let yourself
   be bound by love.
Friendship.

Wisdom
  to learn, to change,
  to let go.
Acceptance
  of the truth
  and beauty within yourself.
Growth.
Pleasure
  in all that you see
  and touch
  and do.
Peace
  with yourself
  and with the universe.

— Maureen Doan

Savor Every Moment

Savor each moment presented to you. Make certain you've taken the time to watch the sun both rise and set and have allowed yourself a moment to enjoy the night light's game of hide-and-seek as the moon and stars peep out of the darkness.

Stop to appreciate the new blossom on a flower as its beauty unfolds and colors the earth.

Be silent and listen to the songs of nature as they greet you. The music of the birds and creatures around us is a gift of Mother Earth.

Smile at the people around you. Be aware that none of us exists within a vacuum and that who we are, what we do, and what we say will have an impact on someone every single day.

Search until you find something good about everyone you come in contact with during your day. It becomes easier with time and practice, and soon you'll see the positive in each person long before you find their faults. And somehow the weaknesses, even in yourself, will seem not so great.

Take a moment, even when you think there is none, to listen to the voice that speaks within you. Let it guide you toward your center and point you toward your future.

Learn to like who you are. We are none without our bad points, but don't allow yourself to focus only on those. Without day, there would be no night. Without cold, there would be no warmth. Without both the good and the bad in each of us, we would exist only as an image and not a real person. Allow yourself to be human — an ever-evolving person — but one with many facets.

Love fully. Love freely. And never regret the emotion. It is the most fragile, yet the strongest, of the threads that weave man's heart.

And, you've heard this before, never put it off. Never fail to tell someone special in your life that they are appreciated. It may not need to be said, but how gracefully it falls on the ears anyway, and how fully it embraces and warms the heart.

— Brenda Hager

May You Find Serenity

May you find serenity and tranquility in
a world you may not always understand.
May the pain you have known and the
conflict you have experienced give you the
strength to walk through life facing each
new situation with courage and optimism.
Always know that there are those whose love
and understanding will always be there, even
when you feel most alone.

May a kind word, a reassuring touch, and a warm smile be yours every day of your life, and may you give these gifts as well as receive them. Realize that what you may feel you lack in one regard may be more than compensated for in another. What you feel you lack in the present may become one of your strengths in the future. May you see your future as one filled with promise and possibility. Learn to view everything as a worthwhile experience. May you find enough inner strength to determine your own worth by yourself, and not be dependent on another's judgment of your accomplishments. May you always feel loved.

— Sandra Sturtz Hauss

Gentle Words
of Encouragement

As you reach forward with one hand, accept the advice of those who have gone before you, and in the same manner reach back with the other hand to those who follow you; for life is a fragile chain of experiences held together by love. Take pride in being a strong link in that chain. Discipline yourself, but do not be harsh. The pleasures of life are yours to be taken. Share them with others, but always remember that you, too, have earned the right to partake.

Know those who love you; love is the finest of all gifts and is received only to be given. Embrace those who truly love you, for they are few in a lifetime. Then return that love tenfold, radiating it from your heart to fill their lives as sunlight warms the darkest corners of the earth. Love is a journey, not a destination; travel its path daily. Do this and your troubles will be as fleeting as footprints in the sand. When loneliness is your companion and all about you seems to be gone, pause and listen, for the sound of loneliness is silence, and in silence we hear best. Listen well, and your moments of silence will always be broken by the gentle words of encouragement spoken by those who love you.

— Tim Murtaugh

May You Find the Peace Within

Every day comes bearing gifts;
hold each promise in your hands.
Within you is your very own universe.
A bit of stardust is blowing your way —
a bit of light and a bit of wonder.
Follow your leanings;
listen to the whispers of your soul.

— Linda E. Knight

May a spirit of grace and gratitude
embrace you in its gentle arms.

May an awareness of
the simple daily pleasures
bless your life at all times.

May you savor the company
    of friends,
the closeness of loved ones,
and the enjoyment of solitude.

May you always appreciate
the quiet routines
constructed with love
that create your life
as you know it.
                    — Virginia Parslow

Acknowledgments

We gratefully acknowledge the permission granted by the following authors, publishers, and authors' representatives to reprint poems or excerpts from their publications.

Shambhala Publications, Inc., for "Within you there is a stillness…" from SIDDHARTHA by Hermann Hesse, translated by Sherab Chödzin Kohn. Copyright © 2000 by Shambhala Publications, Inc. All rights reserved.

Lisa Butler for "Slow Down, Let Go, and Discover Your Inner Joy." Copyright © 2013 by Lisa Butler. All rights reserved.

Lamisha Serf for "Live in the Moment." Copyright © 2013 by Lamisha Serf. All rights reserved.

Gary Seymour for "Life Is Simply a Journey." Copyright © 2013 by Gary Seymour. All rights reserved.

Humanics Publishing Group for "Being calm is easy…" from "Easy" from THE TAO OF CALM by Pamela Metz. Copyright © 2002 by Brumby Holdings, Inc. All rights reserved.

Lisa Crofton for "Listen to your inner voice…." Copyright © 2013 by Lisa Crofton. All rights reserved.

St. Martin's Press for "Beyond your challenges…" from HOW DID I GET HERE? by Barbara De Angelis, PhD. Copyright © 2005 by Barbara De Angelis, PhD. All rights reserved.

Blake Friedman for "There is something greater…" by Kahlil Gibran from THE BROKEN WINGS: A NOVEL, translated by Juan R. I. Cole. Translation copyright © 1998 by Juan R. I. Cole. All rights reserved.

The Elisabeth Kübler-Ross Foundation for "Learn to get in touch with the silence…" by Elisabeth Kübler-Ross. Copyright © 2012 by EKR Family Limited Partnership. All rights reserved.

Counterpoint, LLC, for "The Peace of Wild Things" from THE SELECTED POEMS OF WENDELL BERRY by Wendell Berry. Copyright © 1998 by Wendell Berry. All rights reserved.

Sterling Publishing Co., Inc., for "This is a very short and simple…" and "We can't always be peaceful…" by Ruth Fishel and "Whenever you sense a feeling that…" by Mary Manin Morrissey from PEACE IN OUR HEARTS, PEACE IN THE WORLD by Ruth Fishel. Copyright © 2008 by Ruth Fishel. All rights reserved.

Dialogue House Associates and Jon Progoff, Beachwood, OH, www.intensivejournal.org, for "Mind and body…" from "The Center Point Within Me" from THE WELL AND THE CATHEDRAL: ENTRANCE MEDITATION™ READINGS by Ira Progoff. Copyright © 1977 by Ira Progoff. Reprinted by kind permission of Jon Progoff. All rights reserved.

Heather Parkins for "Sometimes it's the little things…" from "Peace Begins Within." Copyright © 2000 by Heather Parkins. All rights reserved.

Rochelle Lynn Holt for "Take nothing for granted." Copyright © 2013 by Rochelle Lynn Holt. All rights reserved.

Robert Stuberg for "The trouble with so many…." Copyright © 1997 by Robert Stuberg. All rights reserved.

Grand Central Publishing for "Simplicity is different from focus…" from LIGHTPOSTS FOR LIVING: THE ART OF CHOOSING A JOYFUL LIFE by Thomas Kinkade with Anne Christian Buchanan. Copyright © 1999 by Media Arts Group, Inc. Reprinted by permission of Grand Central Publishing. All rights reserved.

Ocean Tree Books for "Inner peace comes through…" from PEACE PILGRIM: HER LIFE AND WORK IN HER OWN WORDS by Peace Pilgrim. Copyright © 1982, 1991 by Friends of Peace Pilgrim. All rights reserved.

The Mono Lake Committee for "The birds and animals…" by David Gaines. Copyright © 2002 by The Mono Lake Committee, www.monolake.org. All rights reserved.

Broadway Books, a division of Random House, Inc., for "To live in a state of grace..." from IF LIFE IS A GAME, THESE ARE THE RULES by Chérie Carter-Scott, PhD. Copyright © 1998 by Chérie Carter-Scott, PhD. All rights reserved.

New World Library, Novato, CA, www.newworldlibrary.com, for "Remember to be gentle…" from LETTERS TO MY SON: A FATHER'S WISDOM ON MANHOOD, LIFE, AND LOVE by Kent Nerburn. Copyright © 1994, 1999 by Kent Nerburn. All rights reserved.

James Bowie for "Relax." Copyright © 1999 by James Bowie. All rights reserved.

The Truth Center, a Universal Fellowship, for "All of us long for peace" from SEIZE THE DAY by W. Norman Cooper. Copyright © 1986 by W. Norman Cooper. All rights reserved.

Sally Clark for "I Remember…." Copyright © 2013 by Sally Clark. All rights reserved.